FROST IN THE
LOW AREAS

FROST IN THE LOW AREAS

poems by

KAREN SKOLFIELD

ZONE 3 PRESS
Clarksville, Tennessee

Book and Cover Design: David Bieloh

Cover Photo: Microscopic view of frost on a blade of grass, by Eric Erbe. Electron and Confocal Microscopy Laboratory, Agricultural Research Service, U.S. Department of Agriculture.

Library of Congress Cataloging-in-Publication Data

Skolfield, Karen.
  [Poems. Selections]
  Frost in the Low Areas : poems / by Karen Skolfield.
     pages cm
  Includes bibliographical references and index.
  ISBN 978-0-9786127-8-8 (alk. paper)
  I. Title.
  PS3619.K64A6 2013
  811'.6--dc23

                            2013036494

Austin Peay State University, a TBR institution, is an AA/EEO employer and does not discriminate on the basis of race, color, national origin, sex, disability or age in its program and activities.

For Dennis, Walker, Felix. Always.

CONTENTS

THREE

INTRODUCTION

Karen Skolfield can muse with brilliant playfulness over almost anything and make it funny or charming or newly charged, or all of these. The homunculus. The skeleton key. The gravelly sound in gracklesong. Car trouble (here things begin to darken). The call of a barn owl that sounds like—could it actually be?—a woman screaming. The LAW (light anti-tank weapon). Trip wire. The Botox mania. And "hunger, always the hunger." Of irony, Rilke wrote, "under the influence of serious things either it will fall from you (if it is something fortuitous), or else it will (if it really innately belongs to you) strengthen into a stern instrument ..." At a certain point in this collection, you feel something fall away, not irony, not Skolfield's wry understatement or her sense of cosmic and cultural dissimulation but some clever, distant, keep-us-in-stitches book this could have been. What remains is the complex, tender and funny/serious book this is, informed by a sense of irony that isn't stern so much as versatile, deft, ethical in its effects.

I'm thinking of a poem like "Army SMART Book: On Being Lost," one of the more striking pieces in this collection. The poem is a parody of a basic training manual for military recruits. (At an earlier time in her life, Skolfield was in the Army; she went through Army basic training and served as a military photojournalist in the National Guard.) Here are the last ten of twenty steps:

> #10: Technically, you're all still children, but soldiers.
> #11: You can't drink or stay out past 2300, but you can shoot people.
> #12: Did your parents sign the standard *in loco parentis* form?

#13: *Loco* also means crazy.

#14: Thank you, Spanish class.

#15: Where it says "you can shoot people," that means people of the Army's choosing.

#16: With no visual cues, subjects will wander in circles as small as 20 meters.

#17: False dawn: caused by sunlight scattering off dust.

#18: How it will make your heart sing. It will feel like first love, imagining the night gone.

#19: Dust rearranged. Light shimmers off. It's you and the dark again.

#20: You're made to look like trees, to disappear.

Comedy, contradiction, danger, information, beauty, camouflage, these are all part of the same knowing that Skolfield articulates so capably; and the poem's final gesture, in which "disappear" hints at obliteration even while on the surface it means "to be safe," feels inevitable, scary and eerily sad.

This is a poet who pays attention to small wonders, who marvels that "sticks / can walk" (the praying mantis) and "the roots of trees gather / forgotten rains," who takes to heart "the river's stillness behind a fallen log," and yearns over human fragility, a child's hand with its "twiggish bones, the little covering of skin." In and around and under the wit these poems are enormously tender. That Skolfield is a loving parent and a spouse everywhere informs the collection. In fact, it is family life that is truly at its center. How fraught it can be. How endangered, and sometimes, how dangerous. In "Rumors of Her Death Have Been Greatly Exaggerated," a mother wonders how to get out of the tangle when, passing a cemetery in the car with her young children, she finds herself explaining methods of burial. How not to say what she is really thinking?

> Shells, mortar rounds, the terror of Claymore mines—

> they're filled with old screws and nuts, metal scraps
> twisting through bodies until they embed deeply
> into trees, even rocks. Someone angry invented

> these, someone who lives in a junkyard.

We see the speaker reaching desperately for images that will reassure and distract her crying son:

> I have both hands on the wheel,
> I'm remarking over the stars, help me look for the moon,
> I'm slowing for a stoplight that is red, red, red, red, red.

Repetition, what Robert Hass calls "the hope of a shapeliness in things," registers differently here to child and adult. Beneath the comfort of shape, a thing seen and known and named and repeated, are associations an adult would have with red—blood, of course, tragedy, and the leap to dead, the obvious rhyme she is willing herself not to say. It's beautifully done. In these poems home is the origin of our strictest taboos and the place they are broken, the place of learning either to look or to look away; of children and parents "lying to each other," of deep affection and intimacy; of strangenesses never quite solved or resolved. Home is the place where

every time I open the freezer
I startle, like the time my daughter
froze her toys, the eyes
of a baby-doll staring, rime-rimmed.

In "Last of a Species," a newspaper clipping about an endangered
bird species has been saved by a harmful parent whose estranged
daughter must grapple with this discovery, must

> ... consider that this man's heart
> was big enough to hold that bird,
> not just for a moment but the time it took
> to get the scissors, to fold the newspaper just so,
> to clip a rectangle, flatten the clipping,
> read it again, think of a place to keep it.

His small act is one the poet doesn't try to account for, one which
coexists with her child's inklings of mortality; our yen for naming
"the dog, the foot bones, the baby, the oak tree"; the body's final
"exchange of calcium for stone"; all the facts we must endure or leave
alone or do with what we can.

"So I have / the LAW on my shoulder and it feels good," says the
17-year-old speaker of "Backblast Area Clear." The light anti-tank
weapon, a "long fiberglass tube, next to weightless," is, once loaded,
"still not heavy, but lethal." Behind the giddiness of a young recruit
with a weapon aimed at a target is the wary voice of an older self who
is troubled by the acronym and how neatly it conceals the seduc-
tiveness of power. (Euphemism comes from the Greek euphemia, or
to use words of good omen!) "'Pretend it's someone you hate,' drill

sergeant says." Mortality, sadness, love, danger, all these are afoot
in Karen Skolfield's poetry. Anything can happen, the news both
good and bad, since we're in it for keeps. In the opening poem, when
the speaker is handed a star that looks suspiciously like a baby—it even
resembles her!—she accepts it, because—Skolfield says this with a playful
archness that doesn't preclude celebration— "If something's held out, /
you can't help but take it in your arms."

Nancy Eimers
Western Michigan University

You must have chaos within you
to give birth to a dancing star.

—Friedrich Nietzsche

I.

WHERE BABIES COME FROM

I thought they were handing me a baby,
but it's a star in my arms, a very small one,
just born. Whoever said they twinkle has never
held one. It's blue and not very warm,
and though I don't know a thing about stars,
I start to worry. I give a tickle, blow on it,
sing a little song, all my tricks. The star
perks up, then settles into me, like it belongs.
Everyone else at the party is clustered
by the hors d'oeuvres. "Hey," I say. "Hey.
I should probably give this nice star back."
Blank looks. "I mean, it's not my star.
It doesn't even look like me." But it sort of does,
right around the edges. So I try again.
"Okay, it does sort of look like me, in the way
that everything in the universe resembles
everything else, in that interconnected way,
you know, a breeze starts in the Horsehead
Nebula and we feel it in Bear's Paw Galaxy.
Or a butterfly is trampled by a horse and..."
I can't remember what's supposed to happen
with the butterfly, but I know it was profound.
They've turned back to the food, what's left
of the warm brie. These are not the people
you want between you and the lifeboats.
A woman approaches. "Cute baby," she says.
She keeps her hands behind her back.
It's instinct, you know. If something's held out,
you can't help but take it in your arms.

HOMUNCULUS

Who doesn't love the idea of a little body
wrapped up in another body? If someone
hadn't already thought of it, I'd invent
the homunculus. I'd put little people everywhere:
not just in sperm, but wood glue, the popcorn
pieces in the couch, the gills of fish, orzo,
pearlescent teeth, navy beans, and of course,
teardrops. Every teardrop would have a little
person, and when the tear splashed down
the person would be free. What I can't decide
is if the person would be a baby or an adult.
Baby problem: no homunculus-sized diapers.
Adult problem: your conscience made real,
or what if you fell in love with that little mite?
Physically, how would you—you know,
split the household chores? Maybe
I'm lingering on details when the big picture
is still pretty cool. Because these homunculi
would honor me as their creator. I'd thought
to put them in the dewdrops, the coagulated
beef grease. They'd hold little parades,
march with their tiny signs bearing aquarelles
of me, shout their thanks, which would sound
like the lazed buzzing of bees. Because
there's so many of them, they'd do all
the things I couldn't, they'd be kinder
and better, they'd have time to pet
all the good dogs, plant more flowers.
There's a swinging contradance band
called Einstein's Little Homunculus,

and when Brendan asked me what that meant,
I told him. How do you know that word,
he asked. I said, I thought everyone knew it.

ART PROJECT: EARTH

Balloon, then papier mâché.
Gray paint, blue and turquoise, green,
a clouded world with fishing line attached
to an old light, original to the house, faux brass
chipping, discolored, an ugly thing. What must
the people of this planet think, the ground
knobby and dry, the oceans blue powder,
the farmland stiff and carefully maintained.
Sometimes they spin one direction,
then back again. How the coyotes howl.
How the people learn to love, regardless.
The majesty of their own towering hearts.
The mountains, which they agree are beautiful.
And the turquoise—never has there been
such a color, breaking into precious
and semi-precious stones. They build houses
from them, grand places of worship,
and there is much to worship. Look up,
for instance. Six suns. The wonder of it.
First one, then the next, eclipsing
the possibility that their world hangs by a thread.

BACKBLAST AREA CLEAR

"I shot one of those," I say to Dennis, pointing
at the screen. It's a light anti-tank weapon,
a LAW, long fiberglass tube, next to weightless.
I was 17 when I picked it up,
drill sergeant beside me on the firing line,
an instructor guiding this gigantic straw onto
my shoulder. Even the small-size uniform
looked ridiculous on me. So I have
the LAW on my shoulder and it feels good.
Not like the M-60, which was like dancing
with a barrel of oil. The LAW was nice.
A little plastic scope pops up, with red lines
and a circle. Downrange, there's a huge
hunk of metal that looks like a tank.
I take off the front cover, a black plastic cap.
Take off the back cover, another plastic cap.
Both swing free. This thing is like a Pixie Stick
it's so light. If I'm ever in a war, I am
definitely carrying one of these, I think.
It's pale green, somewhere between moss
and sand. The instructor loads the thing and now,
it's a loaded LAW, still not heavy, but lethal.
"Pretend it's someone you hate," drill sergeant says.
I'm 17. Firing line clear. Backblast area clear.
Cheek, chin, against the tube. Line up the scopes.
The trigger is under a squishy rubber cap,
not a rifle trigger at all. There's no one
in the tank. Though I'm sure there was noise,

I don't remember it. Just the joy of being
on target, some metal crumbling downrange.
Then it was another girl's turn.
"Did you hit any helicopters?" Dennis asks.
"Don't be silly," I say. "They don't let you
shoot helicopters." But of course, they do.

SECOND HOUSE, CAREFUL IN THE DRIVE

My yard that I love has its own small child.
She loves the sand pile best, the one
I tell visitors came with the house,
isn't it an eyesore, but the kid. I teach her
the words "flick" and "Frisbee."
"Kayak" she already knew. There's one
in my shed turning pink from the light, next to
the wood I can't use, next to the lawnmower,
next to the two bad ladders. The neighbors know
my dog's name and call her as if she's baked
for them or mowed their yard for free.
After a year in the house I've learned
the wildflowers by heart, and I mispronounce
their Latin and study the way leaves clasp
a stem as if the wind might take their ragged hands.
It seems as if everyone but me was born
knowing to hold a child by the wrist instead
of their small, slippery fingers. The distance
from any sidewalk to the whir of cars is exactly one
Emily long. The silky birds arrive and line their nests
with the shedding dog's hair. The rivers tend
to stay put except for that bit in the spring
and the wet basement rug. People wave and loan you
tools here. The saw with the twist of orange ribbon.
Emily can't seem to paint fast enough,
rainbow to rainbow as if the earth might run
out of rainbows and that thick
belt of light. There's so much to know.
Borax to keep out the ants.
When to buy corn. How to hold a hammer low.

Lefty loosey, and the like.
There's a whole set of words not to use
around children. The yard invites a certain amount
of nakedness. The roof is my next project.
Anything I do for this house makes it better
for the next young owners who will,
most likely, have no money but dream
of where to place the hot tub. A previous
owner put a heat lamp in the bathroom. Emily's
pictures go on the wall. She has her own version
of butterflies. Someone planted irises
and oak trees, and this is what we leave behind.

SKELETON KEY

Uses: to enter the castles' creak
and drawbridge, the forbidden throats
of elevators, lockboxes and their forgotten
contents, the unbroken shield of the sky.
A visit to my old apartment
now inhabited by traveling missionaries.
Perfect fit in the palm, the padlock,
it works on any heart, it's a skeleton key,
it unlocks bones and ribcages, untucks tibia
from fibula, talus from tarsals, the bones
of the face, how many there are, how beautiful
they are on you. Even DNA may be unlocked
with secrets from birth and back,
32 teeth for meat and leaves, vestigial gills,
hair everywhere, the curious knuckling of brains
and finally there's a key for it, a way inside
mitochondria, how useful to walk the street
and let free the paving stones, the zoo animals,
the way one person closes himself to another,
a ring that won't come off, a maiden name,
the tight set of lips; unlock wings from birds,
hands from fearful wrists, one half of the leopard
from the other, the warship from its course,
the arrow from its uncertain bow. The criminal
from the crimes. The girl who loves the boy.
The skeleton key from its tarnish, the neck
from its necklace, the bullets from the anger,
the music from its erudition, the lover

from a hipbone, a child from the fall, the stream
from the bed, the power of it, the key in heft
and hand and though it's terrible to say,
the you from me and then we remember
that although the key unlocks
it also binds two things together.

HALA KAHIKI

Overnight, there were pineapples.
The zinnias replaced by pineapples.
Instead of wheat: pineapples. Kentucky
blue grass: you get the idea. If I waited
for the 22, there at the bus stop
were thin little spikes and flowers,
the flowers of pineapples. The sun
stamped red marks over the children's
faces and those, too, were shaped
like pineapples. I put my thumb on one,
I put my thumb on another. "Stop it,"
the boy said, swatting at my hands,
but the pineapples were beyond
my control. The girl's shirt had
pineapples—how did I not notice?
And what else had escaped me?
Someone in my family
was allergic to pineapples,
but I couldn't remember who.
The day was slipping into something
else and the tides were changing
without me. I tried to explain
how the moon and earth love
each other and that's why
we have waves, but clearly
the boy wasn't falling for it.
My husband asked if
I'd noticed all the papaya.
"Those grow on trees," I explained.
"We're talking about something

completely different here."
He whistled something merry
just to show that he could whistle.
I couldn't help but be impressed.
On an island, every step we take
leads to water. He opened his hands
and the fruit tumbled
toward the ripe, heavy ground.

HOW TO LOCATE WATER ON A DESERTED ISLAND

Darling, these are the palm trees
we've endlessly discussed, their closeness
to dinosaurs and leather. Plants produce
spores and send their children in the air.
It's the wrong time to think
of all the houseplants I've neglected, but still.
That night the praying mantis case
hatched in the kitchen: insects so small
and perfect that for a moment we believed
in their prayer. Of course sticks
can walk and the roots of trees gather
forgotten rains. Even science
can't make up its mind about the divining
rod trembling in the old man's hand:
is it the fork or is it his body
endlessly seeking its source? Here shade
has a brand new meaning. An art form
and our bodies bend to fit in the shapes
laid out for us. Rest for a moment my love,
my comma in the dark. The air around us
explodes in plumage. Watch where the birds go.

BIRDS UNLOVED

In flocks the grackles, giant flocks at fall.
No migration but they moved around
in darkening flocks, moving not from cold
but toward greater flocks, merging
into tributaries into rivers into oceans,
from comparative to superlative, grackle sky.
They perched on the forest behind some houses,
replacing the downed leaves, shaking
as if they were leaves, the great noise of them
greater than leaves, their great grackle sound.
And a little grackle girl beneath them,
plain the way the birds were plain,
in the right light shimmering,
small plain body, aerodynamic
but somehow rooted to the ground
beneath the grackles plain.
Their gravel calls in the leafless woods
and dropping gravel grackles,
the autumn cold and cold-blooded grackles
dragging cold behind them, through the gravel.
The girl with her piece of two-by-four
standing on the back deck, the redwood
ringing deck with her board, girl quiet
waiting until all the birds had lit,
thrumming on the trees their grackle leaves,
their birdish sounds, the rudest things
in the woods and all that gravel,
rock-rubbing sounds, the grating of stone chips.
Of course that girl was me, but how hard
to care about her now when there were grackles,

when the thing I have to thank her for
is her fascination with grackles flocking,
for the long pause as she lifts the still-silent
board toward a raucous grackle horizon.
Then brings it clapping down,
flat to the deck, the clarity of it cutting
through grackle and they lift clarity
all at once into a sky that will again turn blue.

ODE TO THE FAN

The only thing smuggled from my parents' house.
Square, heavy, a motor my age, 19, my dad
telling me I was no longer welcome there,
how he hated my life, maybe because
I'd never slept with him. But this
is about the fan, the green fan
that I hid under blankets in the back
of my lover's gigantic truck, in the time before
SUVs when trucks were functional and ugly.
And the hidden fan, my unhappy cat
that had also been kicked out.
That night I slept on the floor of a stranger,
Jen and I on piles of blankets.
It was July and we turned on the fan
and slept in its hum. I think I slept deeply—
why wouldn't I, with life clearing
like the view from mountains? Like wind
I'd created myself? Later I painted
the fan raspberry, a ridiculous color,
and when I plugged it in my new lover
or old lover or whatever would joke
"Where'd you get that fan?"
because they all knew the fan's story,
the famous Skolfield fan, the way my father
held onto old things like hand tools
he didn't have the strength to use
and rotted chair webbing and sawdust,
because maybe there would be an oil spill,
a whole tank of oil, and sawdust's just the thing.
I didn't speak to my family for a long time,

until the cancer thing, and then every time
I saw my father or got him on the phone
he'd say "Have you seen the fan?
The big green fan?" he'd ask as soon
as he heard my voice, as if he'd forgotten
he'd asked before, and this went on
for 15 years, and I'd patiently answer
"No, Dad, I know the fan you're talking about,
I don't have it." Because although he
was patient, I'd learned from him,
I would outlast him, I didn't mind the questions,
sometimes I'd be the one to bring it up:
"Dad, don't you have a fan for this room?
I remember a fan here, green—did it stop working?"
And he'd say "I thought you had it."
And I'd say "Oh, I wish, what a fan. A fan
to end all fans. You should write a poem about it."
Because he used to write, in college,
and told me he'd stopped to have a family.
We would start every visit lying to each other.
I like to think it pains him, the idea
of his fan with me, how I might neglect it,
the gathering rust, the mice delighting in the cord.
Or worse: that I threw it away.
Or even worse: How it brings me pleasure,
the metal blades stronger than today's plastic,
the solid whir of it, sleep-inducing vibrato.
I like to think I'm contributing to his nightmares:
I cherish the fan. It still works. It's that good.

FOSSILS: BLOUNT COUNTY

All day I could sprawl on the gravesites,
bones beneath my bones, and wonder
who is lucky enough to fossilize, how long
that might take, the exchange of calcium
for stone. We say petrifaction
but what we mean is bone reinventing itself,
reverse ossification, the body's last ditch to survive,
give away the flesh, let the cheeks fall away,
the lips, the hair that went gray so early;
give the eyeballs in their gelatinous cups,
give the folds of the neck, the breasts,
the fingers that swelled with age
so that her wedding ring had to be cut off,
the pads of the feet, the belly, anything that sags,
the wrinkles, the freckles. Give the muscles
that held babies, that climbed hills, turned pages,
blinked, stirred, tapped the chalkboard,
we are more than a series of motions,
more than the first film strip zipping past
a dim lightbulb, give the slow-twitch and fast-twitch,
give the expansion and contraction. To be fossils,
the bones must first remove the casing.
Give the skin that was once against my skin.
Give the heart stilled in its slow river. Give
the lungs on their gray and blameless plains.
Give the brain and its ridiculed circuitry.
Let what wants to eat come eat.

PURGA

I like to punish the different body parts.
Right foot shoved out of the sleeping bag
until cold sets in, the constant danger
of the zipper, those metal teeth.
Then the shoulder, the fading heat,
let someone else stoke the fire, how chilled
the shoulder can get, dark side of the moon.
Wait for the blood to slow, for the speech
to grow incoherent. Then the hands
with their wriggling dependents.
Such a small oval of safety and warmth.
If I had to choose, which body part
would I give up, if the sleeping bag
were too small, if my heart could not
keep up? With which of the extremities
could I part? Left hand, that useless
left hand, clumsy with everything, unable
to write its own name, to steady
the baby's head. Or the nose, the lips,
the parts that wear jewelry, the parts
that men love, or women; we know
we live without appendices or tonsils
but our bodies don't know this
in blizzards. Our bodies start at the edges,
go room to room, shutting out lights.
Frost damage leaves the skin black,
a sign the body has let go. Mummy bag
over the head. Baffling, the warmth
at the core. Bring the foot back in.
Let it think the worst is over.

IN AN AMHERST PARKING LOT, ALL SUBARUS ARE BLUE

One of these directions is west
though the sun won't say.
Freeze and thaw rearranges
the fields and houses,
shuffles them like cards. Wind at a scour.
There's a child's hand in each of my hands,
smooth and damp, warm, alive.
The girl says all along, I've held her hand
the wrong way, the hurting way,
and she's just now found the words for it.
Twiggish bones, the little covering of skin.
We differentiate storms by the ability
to do damage. In our yard,
snow pruned a pear sapling
until there's a trunk and no laterals.
How does that make you feel,
I ask snow so guilt-ridden
it's melting, humble at the tree's base.
The sapling in shock, pointing
at the sky, that dark old thing,
torn at the edges, blind eye turned.

OR MAYBE IT WAS THE NAME OF A ROCK BAND

Concrete surround of the city, Milwaukee.
On the sidewalk "We found a dead man"
spray painted multiple times, which means
maybe just what it says. Two guys walking
until they noticed the legs frozen
at a wrong angle. Or a set of eyes, unblinking,
fashioned from glass. A face gray-shaded.
The end of a life when the wind goes still.
And the scene was so powerful
that one man's taken up his spray paint,
unable to shake the image of the dead.
"We found a dead man."
Not "We saw" or "We noticed,"
"found" lays claim,
a finder's keepers, an object of value.

We're here for a wedding, Milwaukee.
It's hard not to let the dead man in,
think of him just outside the Hilton's grandness.
A ballroom, a fleur-de-lis, a chandelier, a dead man.
The spray paint words have made him always dead.
Not a man who could have watched the Brewers,
eaten pretzel bread, done something Milwaukee.
Around the Hilton and for blocks,
"We found a dead man." It's a wedding.
It's a sentence in spray paint. Somehow
they've managed to hold the dead man briefly
and then pass him to me. When I dance
with him, I realize how clumsy I am
by comparison, how my feet

won't follow. "We found a dead man."
Later, we'll head out of the hotel,
step right over those words.

LOST MOUNTAIN

I hate when I misplace entire geographical features.
There was the oxbow, that's understandable,
its meandering ways, how easy to set it
on the countertop or above the fridge
and walk away, then think of it weeks later,
all dried out. Blame my husband, if I can,
since he is forever depositing items on the mantel.

Next the savannah, or really just a portion
of the savannah, I don't want my muddle-
headedness out of proportion, yes it was large
enough for two lion prides and their prey,
but it wasn't the whole thing. Slipped behind
the couch, as savannahs sometimes do,
and it wasn't until the vultures started circling
that I knew, and what a shock then to find
the savannah, which honestly no one had missed,
instead of the ice cap, which we talked about
every day.

The salt flat was not my fault.
And the hills, who can see them through the haze.

Then the volcano, which you wouldn't think
I could lose, what with the accompanying
poisonous gas, molten lava, etc.,
but I have a knack for this, I am forever losing
sunglasses too, how my husband hates that,
since I like the expensive polarized type.

The delta, the river system, the Continental Divide.
The little desert and then the bigger one.
The worried looks on the children's faces
as if I had misplaced the whole world
and lost something that was really theirs.

DON'T RUN INTO A PLANET, AND
OTHER GOOD ADVICE

You put a rock in space and off it goes,
frictionless, a dancer on the waxed floor.
It feels a tug from the planets, cuts its own
little groove. I'm not sure where asteroids
come from: planets colliding? Or bigger
asteroids popping out little asteroids with
little hairless heads, loving them even if they
have no craters, even if they're smooth
billiard balls instead of the usual potato or
hot dog shape, even if a gray circle looks like
nothing but a rock. Since it's my space fantasy,
let's say the male asteroids have to give birth.
Let's say my husband is traveling, and though
I'm not mad, he needs to be punished.
Let's say the male asteroids are big, huge babies
about the whole thing, as if they hadn't been
giving birth since the dawn of time, or before.
Folks, it's called the Big Bang. That must have
spawned asteroids uncountable, like birth spikes
after blackouts or wars or better presidents
are elected, and everyone names their new
little asteroids Obama or Michelle, because
it's a new day, isn't it, and anything can happen.

II.

RUMORS OF HER DEATH HAVE BEEN
GREATLY EXAGGERATED

Mistake one: driving by two cemeteries when the kids
are tired. Mistake two: saying only some people get
buried. Where are the others, my son asks.

So I have to explain cremation. I'm smart enough
to leave out burials at sea, bodies never found,
the yawn of earthquakes, missing children,

teens on spring breaks that never end, bodies hidden,
basements and old barns and attics. What war can do.
Shells, mortar rounds, the terror of Claymore mines—

they're filled with old screws and nuts, metal scraps
twisting through bodies until they embed deeply
into trees, even rocks. Someone angry invented

these, someone who lived in a junkyard.
So I don't say this. All the while I'm trying to change
the subject, get them home. Look at the Christmas

lights, the yellow car, the cement mixer. But where
do you want your ashes, he says, where is it that
you love. He's crying, he's tapping my shoulder,

I'm exclaiming over a stray dog and do you think
we'll get more snow, wouldn't you love more snow
Walker; he's saying when is Daddy going to die,

don't die before me; I have both hands on the wheel,
I'm remarking over the stars, help me look for the moon,
I'm slowing for a stoplight that is red, red, red, red, red.

POWER OUTAGE: 3 P.M., COLLEGE OF ENGINEERING

The rooms now closets, black as the handles
of spades pushing their rude darkness into every
conversation. Engineers make widgets
that alert oncoming deer to cars or oncoming
cars to deer: either way, the one gracefully steers

out of the path of the other. Engineers know
why lights go on and off, something besides
my dim reasoning that light follows the motion
of a hand on the wall, a strange sign language
of cables and conductors, crimps and wire,

my engineering friend holds up copper threads and says
This is how one particle of light talks to another.
The threads glow strangely in his hand.
Digital, he says, knows only how to say yes and no
while analog understands *maybe*.

Even in a power outage folks can be civil
with no undue hand holding though the pupils,
by necessity, drink in what they can.
Ben Franklin, that great and randy inventor,
once said that in the dark all cats are gray.

I haven't found a way to work the word
lesbian into a discussion of power spikes.
There's a whole wing devoted to making
things smaller and faster. There's an unfulfilled deer
running around whose one wish is to take out a car.

Grounded, says my friend, means any object connected
to the earth. He says: Someone is dancing around
the master switch. He says: Knowledge is power.
Arms outstretched, we mince forward, where everything
is ordinary and people wander, wide-eyed, out of the gloom.

STURM UND DRANG

Let's line a room with cinder blocks,
paint them something cheerful
and hang up prints of Sicily. Then add:
oh. Fluorescent lighting. I wouldn't notice
but the students act as if they were being pressed
to death. As if the rest of their lives were cheery
and full of volunteer work and perfect omelettes.
The baby cries her really pissed-off cry,
as if her beachfront property just slid into the sea.
When we speak to infants, we don't use words
like *hemoglobin*, even when the context begs
for it. Also no juggernaut, no etcetera.
$40.01 at the gas pump instead of an even $40.
My niece is sure the world has its thumb
on her scale. Who hasn't had students
weep in their office for being 19?
We say "there there," implying
there might be a better place to cry.
Strangers perfect in their strangeness warn:
my toddlers will turn into teenagers.
My mother-in-law tells me about Indiana
raindrops as if she had bets placed on them.
As if she could change what's blowing our way.
If you cut enough words, it's just a classroom
of us with nothing more to say, but oh,
how I like to wave that red pen around.

$99 BOTOX AT URGENT CARE CLINIC, LOS ANGELES

I want to take a picture of the sign
but I can't convince Dennis
of the worthiness of it, it's fast-food Botox,
it seems so California, certainly worth
pulling over though we're jet lagged
and can't find a restaurant,
does no one eat here, are all their needs
met through Botox and furniture stores,
"Please pull over," I ask.
Dennis lays his hand on mine and says
"Their needs are different from yours."
That's his way, I understand the lesson
but I want to learn California,
I'm from Nowheresville,
I have books for identifying grasses
and sedge, it seems so ridiculous here,
I own rain boots, a snow shovel,
backwoods skis, I'm forty, I'm curious,
who wouldn't be, give me a glimpse,
give me clients, give me $99, the camera,
a few crow's feet, I want to take this
with me, tuck California in a warm pocket,
I'm a country mouse, girl in the woods,
I'm all laugh lines, I'm out of my element,
I'm gaping at the sign and then it's gone
and it's my whole body, sagging.

GIVE YOU GREEN

In all the world, there is this one color
made just for you, for the shadows
you love, and the leaves. We'd do
anything to see some oranges
turn on an orange tree.
What would you be
to me without the grass
staining your knees, and the fire
of your hair? If we began celebrating
every little thing we loved, the feel
of moss and of your hands,
the sound of things dropping
into a well and our throaty imitations,
the place where our mouths first met,
we'd never get any sleep. Inside,
there's a new color waiting. The stones
dipped in the river and lined up
like the busy ellipses. Some people
marry as an afterthought and others
picked their children's names when
they were six. The new wheat wants
so much to be brown and blown
by its own success. Little seed heads
nestled with the other seed heads,
to a horizon filled with what
we expect of farms. If only
we could keep everything just this way.
That old car—which field was it in?
Those grand headlights guarding
what grew beneath.

DREAM HOUSE

for Ali & Jeannette

House bones. Plywood, windows, a roof,
the front door is foam, of all things, a play door,
a door for children. We imagine a kitchen,
sketch the stove on the subfloor, a counter,
a place where food will marinate and stew,
rise and expand, chopping block,
a sink for washing and for turning hands red,
for chapped hands, a counter for soaps and flour,
sugar and nutmeg, teapot, knives. Only one
of them cooks. Where carrots will go. Lentils
and quinoa. The savory and sweet.
Where tile will lie, then grime, then mop.
Children and dog. Then mop again. Where the
good china will one day fall, no one's fault,
but tea-stained chips reappear for years.
Where a boy will learn to cook without help,
sandwiches sloppy with cheese. Where useful
gadgets. Where food. Where another child
might yet be born. The stairs up have
no railings yet, and our kids and theirs
climb without fear, arms wide over
unfinished space, wood raw and vulnerable,
a place where a bedroom will be.
There will be a day just for doors, another
for doorknobs. The children must peer out
each new window, as if January might have ended,
as if watching for changes to come.
The improbable tub. Someone will stand naked
before it, fill it with water and salts, step in,

emerge changed. Then it will be someone else's turn,
someone else's, dirt from the yard and the day,
dirt still in the making, plumbing at the magical cant
so that water rushes down, only down.

HOW STRANGE MIGHT LIFE BE

We've given names to everything, or just about everything.
We fancy ourselves regular Adams and Eves that way.
To the creatures we deem special, we give individual names

like Rex and Teddy. We name the fish in the fish tank
if we can tell them apart, the one missing a fin. Along the way
someone named the dog, the foot bones, the baby, the oak tree.

Someone agonized over Karen Diane and wrote it
on a napkin, in very small letters so the pregnancy
would not be cursed. Karen Diane was the size

of an oyster's pearl and held her brain in her hands.
Karen Diane had eye sockets but no eyes,
and her brain waves, so the studies say, sounded like

balled-up socks in the dryer. The gills come
before the lungs. The hands begin as paddles.
It would be one more child in a world busy

with other things. In 18 years Karen Diane
would argue with her mother about women's rights
and where was the choice or the child and the things

they said out of anger would sit darkly between them.
Adam and Eve named their sons until one killed
the other and after that, the kids were named

with a single letter so as not to take up too much space.
The name "Cain" has never recovered, which makes sense,
nor "Abel," which makes less sense except that we want

our children to be immortal. The fetal heart
has no chambers and no purpose for the first month,
no flutter and no thump-in-time. Karen Diane,

your mother was upset because somehow you'd
grown legs and walked away. At zoos, animals born
in captivity are given names and those from the wild

are not. There are names for fear and sorrow, for mirth,
for peace. "Look," her mother told Karen Diane, "What if
I'd had that choice?" Her right hand gripping hard

on the left. There are names that mean the small joy
of locusts gathering before the storm
or the river's stillness behind the fallen log

or the smell of burning leaves, and names for the trees
that cast those leaves down. "Karen" means "Headstrong."
"Diane" means "Left on shore."

LAST OF A SPECIES

For years my father kept this newspaper clipping:
a photo of a bird, one of the last four known
of its kind, all males, a small bird, goldfinch-sized,
nothing unusual except my dad kept the photo,
this is my dad we're talking about,
a man not exactly lauded for his thoughtfulness.
He kept the photo in the buffet,
a drawer with silver and linens, barely used,
in the dining room that looked out on the woods.
And I have to consider that this man's heart
was big enough to hold that bird,
not just for a moment but the time it took
to get the scissors, to fold the newspaper just so,
to clip a rectangle, flatten the clipping,
read it again, think of a place to keep it.
Or maybe it sat on his desk for a long time
and later, when the four birds were long dead,
he still could not bear to part with the yellowed
newsprint, its particular smell of things gone by.
He moved it to the buffet drawer,
a final gesture, loving even,
the last migration for this singular bird.

CHECKING THAT THE MATTRESS IS
STILL STRAPPED TO THE CAR

That's how the world works: A little mirror
tells you more than you want to know.

Let's say you're moving cross country,
reinventing yourself. You think a cowboy hat
would suit you, or a Nehru collar, a nose ring.

Once a person of your gender
rubbed a hand through your hair and you liked it.
Spent a long time deciding if it
was a "tousle" or a "caress," and what
did it mean that you closed your eyes,

that you close your eyes sometimes and think
of fingers, that happy zing to the brain? The feel
of startled feathers across your scalp?

That's an entirely unsexy word, scalp. Better
to be touched on the cheek, the thigh,
somewhere else in the body's restaurant
that is warm, warm, and strangers lean in
for a smell.

There's a road rick-racked in front,
some big states beyond. There's a mattress
on your car. There's your hair, beneath it.

Sometimes, you reach up to see it's still there.

MOVIE NIGHT

Movie night at Fort Benjamin Harrison,
and what a surprise, someone's again rented
Full Metal Jacket in my barracks.
The connection: a military journalist,
pad of paper tucked into his helmet band,
but why must we preview our lives in combat,
trying to remember the story, where the trip wire
was hung or the placement of tank mines
or who died valiantly and who died with their backs
turned or the blackness of helicopter bellies, really,
what is my job here. By day we learn
to write news leads, press releases, features
for the base paper. We practice interviews,
not interrogation, the more useful military skill.
We roll film onto metal spools and dunk paper
into liquid bins of developer, fixer, the heady
smell of it, tangy, like citrus vinegar, no,
stronger than that, it carries the weight
of sulfur or gunpowder smells
without the associated bullets and flames.
None of us wear gloves, we are journalists,
people of words and photos, and when
someone's hands go to his face
it's to smell the fixer. The nickname
of my journalism teacher is Dr. Death.
If we're ever in battle we will remember
him fondly, his rules of military photography:
Never take pictures of a soldier smoking.
Sends the wrong message. And we get it,
we really do.

MAYDAY

"And if there's no way to radio for help,
use red flares or the SOS signal.
Three taps of metal on metal. S. O. S."
Though he didn't make the sound,
we could all hear the taps in our heads,
hear the exact pitch and call of those taps,
the ringing, the way metal can amplify sound,
send it long distances, S – O – S,
perhaps a shovel against a flagpole,
a wrench against a pipe or one rifle
to another, although how desperate
would you have to be to bang rifles together,
what would have happened, what foxhole
would you be in, would there be a body
next to yours, maybe a little bit alive
but not caring that you were knocking
her carefully sighted scope to shit, because
that sound of metal on metal would be
her last hope, that desperate noise above
the night sounds or maybe hidden
in battle chatter but still you hit
with metal on metal, ammunition case
against canteen, canteen to rations kit,
rations kit to bayonet, one, two, three,
one, two, three, you only have to count
to three but each set seems so long,
so metallic, the helmets now are Kevlar
or you'd use it one, two, three, what a ring
a metal helmet would have, how it would tug
at the ears of someone, a medic nearby,

a priest, maybe she's Catholic, she might be
Catholic, yes, you distinctly remember
that conversation and how you brought up
the priest pedophile thing. And wish
for time to say sorry one, two, three,
your tiring arms and the longer and longer
pauses one, two, three, and now
your signal sounds like metal swinging at air.

THE SOUND UNDER THE CAR CAN'T BE GOOD

A wad of plastic bags melted to the exhaust,
better than when I crushed the tricycle
but still it sounds wrong, a dozen tiny hands
slapping the undercarriage as if children were
there, not children in distress, but children
wanting to be noticed. Someone else's children.
I pull over and they stop. I start
and again, the hands, on the verge of anger,
fists pounding on the door of a person
pretending to be gone. Cold January night.
I could fix this myself, be on my way.
Cherry Hill Golf Course ahead, the only streetlight
flaring sodium pink and I drive slowly,
the hands tiring, the hands giving up hope,
even resting sometimes, children's hands,
palms that will bruise the next day,
a reminder of a woman trying not to hear.

AS IT TURNS OUT

As it turns out, my mom's not dead. I've just forgotten
to call for four years. I've had two kids in the meantime,
my appendix removed. Bought a new computer, a goat.
Learned to make my own yogurt and do some minor
plumbing, no big deal, it was after a party and a guest
stuffed the pipes with something furry.
Thought briefly about changing the spelling
of my name to "Cairn," the stone towers that mark
the hikers' path. Something goofy about finding
my way, though that's not what I'll tell her.
Last summer, shot a rabid raccoon walking
toward me in sunlight. It looked generous
and thoughtful. It looked like it wanted
to be my friend. Cooked a bunch of meals.
Separated the lights from the darks.
Vacuumed. When I finally call we'll feel
awkward and talk politics, home remodeling,
the trip to China that got cancelled,
the price of I don't know. Eventually I'll ask her
about her life, and why did I think she was dead?
What was the whole funeral thing about? It was nice
seeing my brothers. There were some flowers,
people there I'd never met who loved her. They said
nice things. My brothers and I almost held hands.
I'll ask: Was she there, secretly? Disguised
as the young woman in yellow? And the casket:
Stuffed with anise drops, cinnamon Dentyne, what?
I was pregnant with my son, who would be born
on her birthday. There was a reception, too, with food
from the ladies of the church. It's funny, now,
to think how I said no to that second slice of pie.

CHERRIES

Every summer my mother picked cherries
as a child, days of cherries on the farm,
the bucket she wore on a string around
her neck, a bucket always in the stages
of filling. And so she never understood how
my father could like cherries, love them even,
the season of cherries. It was the one thing
she was allowed to hate about him,
openly question. She knew,
she must have known, that he
had raped at least one niece,
granddaughters, the daughters of visiting
missionaries returned from the field.
She said nothing, for years,
kept silent about what she'd seen and been told,
it was the cherries that took the heat
and she refused to put them in bags,
had me do it or sometimes my father,
those thin grocery bags bulging
with dark cherries I had touched
or my father had touched or both of us
scooping them up, feeling for splits or spots
or softness, the stems coming off in our hands.
My mother circling the lettuce, checking oranges.
And so I hid my love of cherries from her
and snuck them in small fistfuls, the surprise
of all that cherry juice and the flesh
clinging to stone, it took the whole body
to eat cherries, lips and teeth of course
but also shoulders hunched, chin jutting,

the eyes searching for my mother's shape
and I do not think I was ever caught.
Or if I was, I'm sure she looked the other way.

SCATTERING

A pan from the drying rack, the hearty slip.
Shattered to four rooms—how can that be?—
wings of glass, briefly airborne, the sound
of the whole morning changed.
Diamonds glittering in the grout, the chaos
of dogs and vacuum cleaner.
We carry the kids to high places
as if the shards were mice
gunning for their legs. Cartoon through
the rooms with broom and dustpan.
Vacuum each other's shoes,
the kitchen's secret places.
Kids make catwalks from couch to hearth,
oblivious to jagged glass near bare feet.
They're little and do not know what Dennis
and I know: this house is no longer safe.
And by extension: the world is covered in glass.

III.

HAVING SECRETLY GIVEN EACH OTHER
THE TITLES OF BIRDS

This is the day where longing flies from the hands like a dove,
the knowable bird, dirty as pigeons but deemed lovable,
carved into the backs of furniture, their necks into hard hearts
of wood. Somewhere there's a well capped in your lawn.

Stones cold to the somewhere water's dark throat.
Birds have regions and territories, and songs all their own.

Bones empty with flight.

Somewhere in their nougat of brain birds mate for life,
memorize her particular thatch of pintails, the beak's errant dot.
A birthday. A way of taking coffee.
A dove in mourning will hopscotch
the passing cars' tires if its mate has been struck down
by a wayward fender, a dove in mourning will shed actual tears,
it will wipe them with a handkerchief the size of a coin.
Not all of this appears in the book.
A dove will nest in the hair of the singular.

Birds too yellow to be doves.

And at the window you pull the crisp pages,
page after page of want, putting a name on everything.

LAZARUS SPECIES

I.

Of all the dinosaurs, I miss Spinosaurus the most.
A meat eater, I love their bigger brains,
their sense of resolve, the loose idea
of camouflage, keeping 20 tons still
except for two great, blinking eyes. The sail of bone
along its back and the debate about color
and purpose, an early art form, a way
of attracting mates, probably mates based on
our own flashiness, the way we signal with eyes
and hips, the little Cenozoic strut. We're not related
except for the hunger, always the hunger.

II.

Then the terror birds ruled. Ten feet tall,
flightless, dreadful curved beaks,
the speed of antelopes, carnivorous.
Dinosaurs I might have outwitted.
Terror birds, no. There's one circling
my little hut, afraid of nothing, cutting a swath
through the grasses, not caring that I'm a mammal,
I'm something new with a huge brain,
the ability to tie knots and whistle,
write my own name, play thumb wars,
use rocks and sticks for tools,
observe and remember, form family units,
follow two-step directions, extrapolate, theorize,
way more verbs than this bird, outsource,

relax, minimize, offload, consolidate, oh the list
of what I can do, I can yell for help in what will be
a very small voice.

III.

Also I miss the whole Pleistocene, wooly mammoths
rubbing their great shaggy backs together,
waiting to see what trick I would produce next,
if I would bring fire.
The dire wolf, their packs shrinking, the scarcity
of pups, the old thought *I wouldn't sleep with him
if we were the last two on the planet.*
She knew she'd be the last skull in the fossil record,
the very last to hang on some wall,
and every once in a while some new species
would think to brush off the dust.

IV.

And then: did you know I'd come to this?
The ivory billed woodpecker. This thing is gigantic,
otherworldly, size of a large housecat
but a bird. Was gigantic. Or is, because
some scientists and birders are convinced
there's a breeding population in Arkansas.
Reclusive, stubbornly aloof. And I must consider
the desire, these scientists and hobbyists
that love a species enough to call themselves
after it, birders, to name themselves
based on another animal, to imagine
the hollow bones and feathers

of a species long thought extinct,
surviving somehow, it would be
like living in a small town, all the ivory bills
nodding at each other, aware of each other's
business, keeping a sharp eye for ivory bill
infractions, the misdemeanors of youth,
the preening, the cat-calls, the small-town fears.
If it's been 30 years since we've seen ivory bills,
it's been 30 years since they've seen us.
The inbreeding, the intrigue.
Something forgotten may one day
walk out of these woods.

IN THE HOUR WHEN THE ROCKS SLEEP

In the hour when the rocks sleep
soft in the dirt of small rocks sleeping,
and toadstools begin their thin fractions of lives
the barn owl screams a woman's scream
and we wake, no longer safe with a scream
from the woods, and all the rocks,
and the darkness that we loved before growing darker
and the stars no help at all, beautiful but no help,
there is a woman screaming and the skin's nerves
tangled on the skin, in shock, the blankets snarled
and the blockade of ordinary things, the transformation
of dressers and rug edges, there is a woman screaming.
"Something's wrong"—and Dennis moves as if
he'd been waiting, as if he knew the woman
was there, hurting, gathering her breath in the dark,
knowing she had one last scream in her and the sound
startling even her who has not heard her voice
in too long and cannot remember sunlight or the smell
of anything but leaves in layers, molding, fresh on top
but descending to the richness of decay. This is what
waits for us. It was a barn owl calling first
from the woods and then the front yard's hemlocks,
a woman's cry, it must be her last cry, and the owl's wings
beat their silent flight around our unfamiliar lives.
We wait on the back porch, under the weakness
of porch lights and lopsided robes and listen,
we are her last hope, listen for her calling us.

NEW MOON: RUPERT, VERMONT

The feel of a penny in a dark purse.
The feel of fingers in gloves, body
in jacket, toes against wool, tongue
against teeth, lips against air.
Small body against large body.
Frost sounds. Someone else's forest,
shape of a windmill against the pitch,
barn hulking windward, wind its own
secret color. You think you know black
but don't, each object shifting to smoke,
one thing blending to the next, to the trees,
unlit cabin, the hooded sky. The dogs
bounding by, snow-crust, gift of second sight,
our once-pliable bodies growing stiff
as if these were our last moments, rhythm
of boots boots boots. Bushes without shape.
Shapes firm at a distance, then dissolving.
Too dark to say much. Stars that won't stop.
Hole in the sky where clouds fall through.
Place where a moon should be. Great eye
winking shut. Wood for the woodstove.
Turn on the headlamps and erase the stars.

AFTER MAKING A WRONG TURN I BECOME STUBBORN
AND PRETEND TO KNOW THESE BARNS

And why couldn't these barns be my barns,
known barns, chipped red because when
might farmers find time to paint barns,
what moment of their day is not consumed
with seed and something's terrible thirst?

And why couldn't I know the cows on the left,
one banging her head on the mended fence
she's broken through before, walked across
the road, banged her way through the next,
into the next set of cows, the next reddened barn?

I know her wandering from barn to barn,
how we live in a state of unlost, hoping
for the rare moments of meander, the times
our feet turn toward someone else's barn,
how we lower our heads and charge on.

And why couldn't I wait for the farmer whom
I don't yet know? Why couldn't I ask him
how the roads return? At the end of the day
someone will hold the barn door open
for those cows, knowing they'll come home.

IN UPSIDE-DOWN WORLD, ADULTS LIVE LIKE TODDLERS

Because everything must be tasted, the day starts early.
Long fingers inserted in capricious jaws.
Startling to learn what is part of your body, and who,
the way someone else's hair can blind you,
here is a hand, it is your hand, you must be quick,
ferocious, you must roar with your thick, dumb tongue.
Though the food comes prepared, it's all
white and orange. You live in passive tense.
So sad to learn that couches are for sitting.
Something's gone wrong with your internal ear,
and you must think: leg, other leg, leg.
Pinwheel of arms. The long and terrible fall.
Stairs impose a special hazard. The doorknobs
you may never reach. Across the street,
the glittery objects beckon. Tears come easily:
The world so beautiful and your gigantic heart,
how could you not be moved. Sleep against your will.

WHILE PEELING A BANANA

I rip off the stem and send it sailing across the room.
That's how strong I am, how very unstoppable,
the others here have quit their chatter
and look at the banana stem brought low,
look at me. I feel their envy and fear.
"She looks like a 40-year-old woman,
but what else can she do?" I consider
following up with the coffee cup, the table
with its surprising picture top of Love-Lies-Bleeding,
my backpack that I can't help calling a bookbag,
so old-school am I. Still, check out these biceps,
these gams. Maybe the other patrons
feel safer with me around: who else
to wrestle the crazed gunman to the ground,
take back the purse from the petty thief,
help the elderly across the road?
I'm your gal. Give me the car to lift
off your infant. Give me the house's center beam
so bowed in by snow. The barn sagging
toward its worried cattle. The well to dig,
the surprising boulder, the things that once
seemed unmovable, the game-enders.
Tree In The Road, what can I say?
In just a moment I'll give your trunk
the special hug, a grunt from deep within,
lift with the legs only and send you flying,
startled, back the way you came.

HEAD INJURY GUIDELINES

What's your middle name, what timezone
is Madagascar in, when did Delaware
join the Revolution, what's the name of the dog
your father loved, what's the secret you're withholding.

And now we will shine a light in your eyes,
we will put our face close to your face, we will
touch foreheads, until we've gotten quite
carried away and your pupils cut their own orbits.

If we say "Stand on one foot," we mean "It's time
for some answers." If we say "Touch your nose,"
we mean "Hold my hand." If we say "Tell me about
the accident," we mean "Why don't you kiss me anymore."

The queasiness, normal. Also the urge to flee,
the sudden updraft of love, the butterflies on your
fingertips, the floating dark spots, the halo
around lights at night, only at night.

Moon synapses, normal. The starlight's tapestry.
The weft of streetlamps with their rainbow aureoles.
Your sudden urge to sing. The cerebral cortex wrinkling
and unwrinkling. A new world revealed only to you.

In the morning, you'll have trouble waking.
Isn't it lovely, the blur at the edges? The newest neurons
carting away the old. The lost love relived, the indistinct
purpose, the intake of broth, how we envy you.

DISPOSAL

I.

The things we once loved,
the cracked and tarnished,
the black pumps with the broken heel,
cane chair unraveled, nicked Mason jars.
Trash must be double-bagged
though the sign doesn't say why.
The half-lives of plastic. We recycle,
we have a compost bin loved by bears.
We have a way of letting things go.

II.

The note said that my pea seeds
are infected with pea weevils, many
apologies, here's a refund, be sure
to incinerate the seeds. So the seeds sit
now in my freezer, under the assumption
that weevils need a little warmth
to hatch. They're next to a big hunk
of meat and every time I open the freezer
I startle, like the time my daughter
froze her toys, the eyes
of a baby doll staring, rime-rimmed.
I'm not sure how to incinerate hard peas,
if I can boil them, if a small fire will do,
if I must clear the driveway and start
a bonfire, let it rage and rage, the pea seeds
warming in my hands, in my too-warm hands.

III.

Home canning: Vegetables that
have spoiled must be disposed of
so that no animal or person can touch it.
Not just eat it, but touch it,
because sometimes the bacteria
have all the power, our bodies
giant fortresses with the drawbridge
down, the windows flung wide,
the guards asleep or almost asleep.

IV.

If bears can smell three miles
how deep must the disposal hole be?
I would dig until my shoulders ached,
until the muscles popped, the sweat rose
along the seams, the skin crackled;
I would dig to bedrock, to the water beneath,
to the fossil layer, the imprints of ferns,
I would devote my life, pass through
the colored bands, the place where oil
is made, until the ground grew warm
and when I looked up, the top of the hole
would look like a distant, futile star.

SPACKLER'S LAMENT

All over the city, pockmarks in cement,
imperfect surfaces, macadam's undulations,
rounded edges where hard corners should reign.
Stop signs with bullet holes. Loose screws
at the playground: holes-to-be. Bee hives,
doorways that never close,
the space between bars at zoos and jails,
the madness of chain-link fences.
Certain yoga poses. Windows rolled down,
someone beautiful leaning out
of the taxi, calling in Spanish or Catalan.
Clouds torn by the wind and patched again;
above that, faint craters of a daytime moon.
The country's no better. Ragged shagbark,
the emptiness formed by a squirrel's tail
touching its back, holes in the snow,
the indentation made before the seed drops in,
the very thought of seed cavities, blue bottles
lined up on a windowsill, your windowsill,
in the country, your face with a mouth.
Victorian trim. In the yard, a girl's hands
cupped around broken blue eggs, guarding
only the speckled idea of the bird.

Step #1: Berate yourself for not taking a buddy to go pee.

Step #2: Don't panic. You may choose to a) yell and wake up one of the other girls or b) stay quiet, embarrassed to speak. With option b, move deeper into the woods.

#3: It's your first time away from home.

#4: When your toes hit the ocean, you'll know you're screwed.

#5: You're in camouflage but want to be found.
Isn't that funny? C'mon, it's funny.

Step #6: Leaves at night feel like little hands.

#7: That's a lot of little hands.

#8: The enclave of tents should be at irregular spacings through the trees. Don't make it easy on the enemy.

#9: Or each other.

#10: Technically, you're all still children, but soldiers.

#11: You can't drink or stay out past 2300, but you can shoot people.

#12: Did your parents sign the standard *in loco parentis* form?

#13: *Loco* also means crazy.

#14: Thank you, Spanish class.

#15: Where it says "you can shoot people," that means people of the Army's choosing.

#16: With no visual cues, subjects will wander in circles as small as 20 meters.

#17: False dawn: caused by sunlight scattering off dust.

#18: How it will make your heart sing. It will feel like first love, imagining the night gone.

#19: Dust rearranged. Light shimmers off. It's you and the dark again.

#20: You're made to look like trees, to disappear.

OTHER PEOPLE FANTASIZE ABOUT BIG BOATS

I have fantasies about going back to work,
when Felix is in school, and so I buy nice
work shirts now, with buttons and collars.
I'll have this shiny, long desk that I swear
I'll keep clean. Labels, manila folders.
A whole way of organizing with colors.
A phone, an extension, a window that opens,
something nice out the window, a tree,
flowers that the secretaries tend
but no one knows the names of.
True blue flowers, which are rare.
A boss that appreciates me, I mean,
is crazy about me and my work,
calls me her "little gipper," whatever
that means, I don't ask. Home in time
for the kids to get off the bus
and tell me how happy they are
in school, mostly due to their early years
at home with me. That's not too much
to ask. We'll hug, have snack. It's like
we never left each other, only better.
I'll tell them about my day, too,
my big project, some big phone call,
a nice big raise. I'll tell them about
my office, my cube-mates whom I adore,
a picture of Dennis and the kids on my desk.
A chair with lumbar support. Smells of ink
and glue. A yellow stapler worn smooth
by my stapling hands, how I love to staple.
Papers attached firmly, forever, to each other.

IF WE'D CRIED, I WOULD HAVE MENTIONED IT

I've realized I don't keep much
of my mom around. An ornate bottle,
a serving platter, one picture
on the side of the fridge.
We look a lot alike. Everyone said so
at the funeral, which is a strange
time to say that: You look so much
like your mother, who is now dead.
We were the same height for a long time,
and then she shrank, and shrank
some more, and I knew she was leaving.
Short fingers. Farsighted. I'm graying
the same way she did. She was in the ground
by the time we arrived in Tennessee.
On a hillside where it looked like no one
had ever been. Even the new dirt looked
like old dirt. Cold, but only Tennessee cold.
I was six months pregnant, and I wore
a maternity vest designed just for funerals
when you are six months pregnant.
Dark on dark, a pocket for what grows inside.
A little zipper that gave my hands
something to do. My brothers said
I looked nice pregnant, and I believed them.
We milled around the dry December grass,
churning the spent seed heads, and talked
about mom as if she still might show up
with a baked ham, some warm bread.
We were a family raised to believe
in things unseen. Just the one tombstone.

Pink granite. Or maybe it's called red granite,
but it looked pink, and we talked about it
for a long time, the area famous for its quarry.
Hearts and her name, precisely carved flowers.
What I wanted to tell my siblings was that
the wrong parent died. I thought this over
and over, and found some strange comfort there.
Maybe they thought the same thing.
My oldest brother's girlfriend said
"Isn't it amazing what they can do with lasers,"
and I told her about my surgery.
No more glasses. Until then,
I'd let everyone wonder what miracle,
what divine hand, had touched my eyes.

CHIROMANCY

There's a new line on my left palm
from thumb almost to wrist. Knife slip.
Part of it bled but the rest is dry riverbed
as if I'd run out of blood, as if the drought
and famines had come, as if the ocean
receded and kept receding, rows of beach houses
left inland and dry. I was cutting an avocado
at a campsite in California, which wouldn't
be exciting except the avocados there cost
25 cents, which is enormously exciting
to those on my coast. So this line has joined
the other lines on my palm, my heart line
longer than life, the warble of fate,
future in a skinfold, past tucked in
the simian crease, the stubborn head,
the planets in my hand. Below this,
veins that appear more blue each year,
the skin thinning, the lungs filling a little less
and now there's another line to consider,
perhaps it is my Swiss Army line
or Who Taught You to Hold a Knife line
or You Think That's Bad, You've Got
an Artery About an Inch Away line
and the new line pointing to the artery,
the wrist's soft pulse so loved by the suicidal
in their warm baths, they must be
more committed than I, with more
on their minds than inexpensive avocados
and a little boy looking on, "Mommy
did you cut yourself?" and I dropped

the knife and the fruit, luckily not on my foot
because I wasn't certain which
had wounded me, so fast and sure
it might have been the avocado lashing out
and I stared at them both, pinching shut
this new open part of me, this new access point
with blood scarletting in the air, what joy
to be blood escaped and sun-filled at last,
satiated, set free, and to distract my son
I thrust both hands under the picnic table
and said "Did you know that *knife* is one
of those funny words that starts
with a silent k, like knight?" And he said
"You mean knight like a warrior knight
or like the night when it's dark?"
For a long moment I held
one bloodied hand in one uncut hand,
and for the life of me couldn't remember.

FOR PEACE OFFERINGS, YOU HAVE TO BAKE IT YOURSELF

You have to crack the eggs one at a time.
With a fingertip, pick out shells if there are shells,
the visceral white and yolk,
almost but not quite the makings of life.
Toss the shells to the dogs waiting patiently.
Listen for the grind of their carnivorous teeth.
Flour must be sifted, and you have a sifter,
an old one. Metal grate with a metal bale,
a wooden knob for turning. Of course, it was
your mother's. Maybe no one sifts flour anymore.
Maybe you're the only one left.
The sifter makes a most pleasing sound.
The sound of a woman working alone.
The flour grows in a perfectly conical pile, no matter
if your wrist shakes, if your eyes flicker to the clock.
Peace offerings take more time. Melt the butter
slowly, in a small pan, over low heat. It's easy
to think about something else, and burn the butter.
You must stay firm. Stir as if nothing else mattered.
Add sugar because you want to make things
sweet again. Add chocolate if you were in the wrong.
Nuts if you slept with your friend's husband.
Vanilla because it's the one thing everyone loves.
When you present your peace offering, hold it
in front of you. Knock on the screen door.
Say nothing. She'll sit with you on the front porch.
When she lifts a slice to her mouth, do the same.
Let her break the silence. She was raised the same way
you were. You know she'll have to say it's good.

ROCK HALL HARBOR, PENCIL AND
ACRYLIC, UNFINISHED

The blue comes down this way, deliberate,
a light fractured by birds, clouds
on their way, the feel of far-off rain.

In the foreground a boat still in pencil.
The bones of it, the hull in pieces though
the curve's there, a hatchmarked stern.

The artist put down his pencil, his brushes.
Walked away or died. Began seeing the desert
in things instead of the wet.

Or considered it done, perhaps.
A horizon being built. A boat
in the reckoning. A scene

completed by the viewer's mind,
our willingness to read over missing words,
create what is only suggestion.

I can't remember which lover
I bought this for or how the painting
ended up with me. By now I've grown

used to the changing forests,
the buildings razed, the rope swing gone.
The painting has survived every move,

every awkward swaddling, the time
in all those attics and how surprised I am
at each unveiling, finding something still undone.

FROST IN THE LOW AREAS

The health survey said
he would live to 76 and I, 86.
Something to do with men's

hearts on their worn old grapevines.
Something to do with their will
to lay down and die. In the westerns,

how glad they were to give their lives
away. Bad guy, if you can't shoot down
a junebug's nostril, you don't stand

much of a chance. Men, thinking
they don't have to cut power
to a bound-up sawblade.

Just think, Dennis says. Ten years
to yourself. No one stealing
the sheets or the last of the ham.

He says this as we make pesto.
This is how we joke with
each other, ha ha, and then

we kiss. Seriously, he says,
imagine no more socks
on the mantel. My arms

the sharp odor of garlic. Basil.
Parmesan cheese. Tonight,
a frost the herbs

won't survive. Twilight
we worked the rows,
frantic, our gentleness gone.

Behind us, nothing but stems
and their faint heat. Before us,
the first crisp morning.

ACKNOWLEDGMENTS

Grateful acknowledgment is made to the editors of the following publications where these poems first appeared:

The Adirondack Review: "Or Maybe It Was the Name of a Rock Band," "The Sound Under the Car Can't Be Good"
The Apple Valley Review: "In Upside-Down World, Adults Live Like Toddlers," "Second House, Careful in the Drive"
The Bakery: "Lazarus Species," "While Peeling a Banana"
Barnwood Poetry Magazine: "New Moon: Rupert, Vermont"
Barrow Street: "In an Amherst Parking Lot, All Subarus Are Blue"
B O D Y: "Purga"
BOXCAR Poetry Review, 2011 Best of the Net Anthology: "Rumors of Her Death…"
Cave Wall: "How Strange Might Life Be"
Cider Press Review: "Scattering"
Common Ground Review: "Give You Green," "Hala Kahiki"
Conte: "Sturm und Drang"
failbetter.com: "Chiromancy," "If We'd Cried, I Would Have Mentioned It"
Fiddleback: "Having Given Each Other the Titles of Birds"
Memorious: "Backblast Area Clear," "Mayday"
PANK Magazine: "Power Outage, College of Engineering, 3 p.m."
Rattle: "Ode to the Fan"
The Schuylkill Valley Journal: "Cherries"
Slipstream: "As It Turns Out"
Split Rock Review: "Fossils: Blount County"
Sugar House Review, Verse Daily: "Frost in the Low Areas"
Superstition Review: "Lost Mountain"
Swarm: "Homunculus"

Tar River Poetry: "After Making a Wrong Turn I Become
  Stubborn…"
Thrush Poetry Journal: "How to Locate Water on a Deserted
  Island"
UCity Review: "$99 Botox," "Army SMART Book," "Checking
  that the Mattress…," "Dream House," "Movie Night…,"
  "Skeleton Key," "Spackler's Lament"
Used Furniture Review: "Disposal"
Valparaiso Poetry Review: "Art Project: Earth"
Zone 3: "For Peace Offerings…," "Rock Hall Harbor…,"
  "Where Babies Come From"

Deep gratitude to my teachers, especially Irene Long, Christopher
Buckley, Dara Wier, James Tate.

Additional fist bumps and other in-vogue signs of thanks go to
my two writing groups who have sustained me through words and
amazing meals: Lynette Baker, Kristin Bock, Corwin Ericson, James
Grinwis, Daniel Hales, Liz Hughey, Chris Janke, Daniel Mahoney,
Janel Nockleby, Andrew Varnon; Kristin Bock (again!), Pam Burdak,
Carrie Comer, Caroline DuBois, Robyn Heisey, Caroline Lewis, Judy
Nacca, Sam Wood.